Making Masks

Pat Hughes

Nelson

Contents

Masks	4
How to make Masks	5
Painted Masks	6
Paper Plate Masks	8
Eye Masks	10
Balloon Masks	12
Adding Bits and Pieces	15
Glossary	16

Masks

The first masks were made from heads of animals. Hunters wore them when they hunted animals.

In Ancient Egypt, human and animal masks were used when people were buried.

Today, people wear masks on special occasions. They wear them at carnivals, dances and for sport too.

How to make Masks

The next pages will show you how to make some masks.

Make sure you can breathe through a mask. Don't put it on if you can't breathe through it.

Painted Masks

You will need:

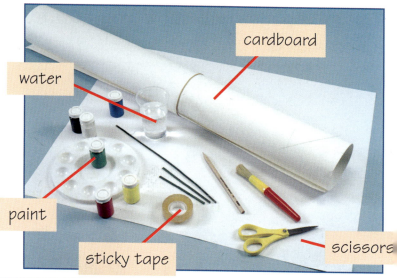

cardboard
water
paint
sticky tape
scissors

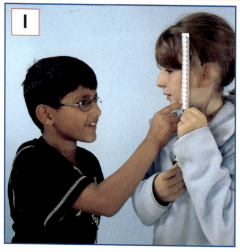

Use a ruler to measure the position of your ears, eyes, nose and mouth.

Draw some mask faces on a large sheet of cardboard.

Paint them with bright colours.

Cut out the holes for the eyes. Cut out the mask.

Hold the masks in front of your face.

Paper Plate Masks

You will need:

- egg boxes
- paper plates
- scissors
- glitter

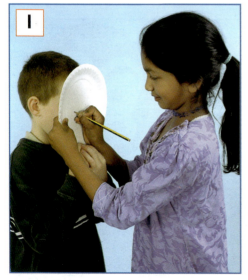

1. Make two marks for the eyes.

2. Push a pencil through the paper plate to make the eye holes.

Attach string to fit your head.

Paint the face.

Add coloured paper, silver stars and pieces of egg carton to make a sun mask.

Eye Masks

You will need:

glitter, paint, water, string, feathers

1. Draw the shape of the eye mask. Cut out the mask.

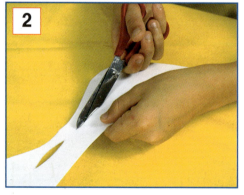

2. Hold the mask in front of your face to mark the position of your eyes with a pencil. Cut holes for the eyes.

Make holes in the side with a pencil and tie the elastic through the holes.

Paint the mask with bright colours.

Decorate the mask.

Balloon Masks

You will need:

- newspaper
- bucket
- wallpaper paste
- balloon

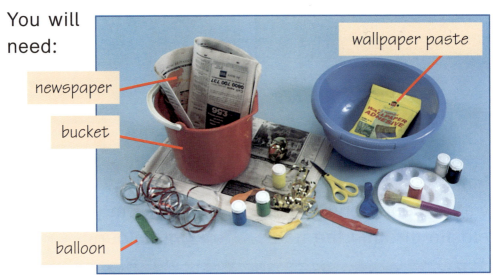

1 Blow up the balloon. Tie a knot at the neck. Stand it in a small plastic bowl.

2 Tear the newspapers into strips.

Put the wallpaper paste into a bucket.

Soak strips of newspaper in the paste.

Cover the balloon with the strips. Give the balloon five layers of newspaper. Let it dry.

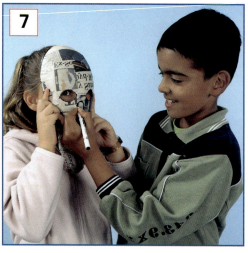

Cut the covered balloon in half.

Mark the position of your eyes, nose and mouth and cut them out.

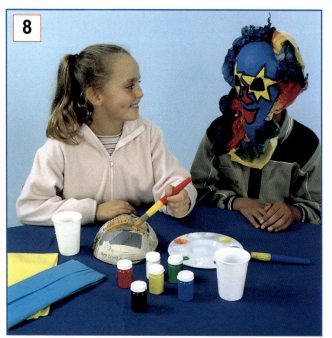

Paint and decorate your mask. Add string or elastic to fit your face.

Adding Bits and Pieces

Collage
Try adding feathers, tissue paper, seeds, woodshavings, or glitter and silver stars.

Hair and Beards
Cut thin strips of stiff paper. Roll them round a pencil.

Glossary

bright – shining strongly

carnival – a procession often in fancy dress with music and dancing

collage – when things like bits of paper, glitter or shells are stuck onto something

decorate – to make something look nicer

knot – to tie together two pieces of string

measure – to find the size of something

strip – a long narrow piece of anything

wallpaper paste – a liquid for sticking wallpaper on walls